LOGICAL FALLACY MONSTERS

An illustrated collection
of logical fallacies

by
Blique

Special thanks to everyone who helped make this book.

This book is dedicated to those doing their best to fight these monsters every day.

Table of Contents

Foreword

This book is about the monsters that lurk in people's minds.

As you go through life and talk with others, you'll encounter people with different viewpoints and different ways of expressing them. It's good to listen to them and understand how others think, as it can open your mind up to new possibilities.

Oftentimes, however, a person may say something strange. It sounds right, but something just doesn't add up. There's something illogical about it, but you aren't sure what it is. Chances are, this is a little monster playing tricks on you: a logical fallacy.

I wrote this book because I see so many logical fallacies in day-to-day life, and so many people who don't know much about them. I want to help more people get interested in logical fallacies, to be able to see them in conversations, on television, on the internet, and to be able to identify them rather than fall prey to their tricks.

I imagine logical fallacies as little creatures in your head, trying to get you to make mistakes. They are the little parts of your brain that may get tricked and lead you to believe what they want you to. This book, this guide to spotting those monsters, can help you realize when one of them is getting ready to strike or has already struck, so you can be ready and keep your thoughts in line with logic.

Logical fallacies are a fun part of learning about logic, and while they certainly are not the end-all to understanding the subject, they are a nice introduction to it. Many of the examples in this book are silly and exaggerated on purpose just to demonstrate the fallacy, so don't take them too seriously. I hope that this book will inspire an interest in logic and philosophy, and help you to understand the world around you just a little bit more.

Introduction to Logic

A **claim** is a simple statement or assertion. It can be fact, opinion, true, or false. Examples of claims:

"Today is sunny with a light breeze."
"Aliens are real and have already landed on Earth."
"Studies show that watching cat videos is good for your health."

An **argument** is two or more claims—premises—that are organized in a way that supports another claim—a conclusion.

$$
\begin{array}{ll}
\text{Premise} & \text{(claim)} \\
+ \quad \text{Premise} & \text{(claim)} \\
\hline
\text{Conclusion} & \text{(claim)}
\end{array}
$$

An argument's form can be represented as:

If P, then Q.
P.
Therefore, Q.

P is known as the **antecedent**, or the first half of a conditional statement. **Q** is known as the **consequent**, the latter half. Here is an example of an argument set up this way:

Premise: If the weather is nice, then I will go outside.
Premise: The weather is nice.
Conclusion: Therefore, I will go outside.

An argument does not always have to be phrased exactly like this. The point is that arguments can be simplified down to this basic structure or to similar structures. These structures are useful when analyzing logic and fallacies.

Deductive Arguments

In a **deductive argument**, the conclusion can be **deduced** from the premises.

Deductive arguments are made using **formal logic**, and are "airtight", foolproof.

Validity and **soundness** are the two criteria used to evaluate a deductive argument.

In a **valid** argument, the premises must guarantee the conclusion.

> *Premise*: If a pet has fur, I am allergic to it.
> *Premise*: All pets have fur.
> *Conclusion*: Therefore, I am allergic to all pets.

While this argument is valid, the information that it contains is unsound, or untrue, because not all pets have fur. A valid argument does not need to be true; it only requires that the premises prove the conclusion.

A **sound** argument must be valid, and the premises must be true.

> *Premise*: If a pet has fur, I am allergic to it.
> *Premise:* Some pets have fur.
> *Conclusion*: Therefore, I am allergic to some pets.

A sound argument is both valid and true, and therefore cannot be wrong. A sound argument is considered the ideal argument.

Inductive Arguments

In an **inductive argument**, the conclusion can be **inferred** from the premises.

Inductive arguments are made using **informal logic**, and are not "airtight".

Strength and **cogency** are the two criteria used to evaluate an inductive argument. They are similar to validity and soundness.

In a **strong** argument, the premises must, to some degree, lead to the conclusion.

Premise: Sneezing when near fur is a symptom of allergies.
Premise: I once sneezed when I came near an animal with fur.
Conclusion: Therefore, I am allergic to fur.

This argument is not completely airtight, but the premises do potentially lead to the conclusion. However, it is possible that the arguer is jumping to conclusions after just one sneeze. While this argument is inductive, its strength is weak.

A **cogent** argument must be strong, and the premises must have a high likelihood of being true.

Premise: Sneezing when near fur is a symptom of allergies.
Premise: I sneeze every time I come near any animal with fur.
Conclusion: Therefore, I am allergic to fur.

A cogent argument is both strong and likely true, and therefore is a good argument, even if not an ideal one.

Logical Fallacies

A **logical fallacy** is a faulty or badly constructed argument.

Fallacies can be categorized in many different ways. Because fallacies are arguments, one common way is to divide them between formal (deductive) and informal (inductive).

Formal logic refers to an argument's form, so a **formal logical fallacy** is an argument that is faulty because its premises are invalid or unsound. It is an incorrect attempt at a deductive argument.

Informal logic refers to an argument's content, so an **informal logical fallacy** is an argument that is faulty because it is weak or uncogent. It is an incorrect attempt at an inductive argument.

There are different variations of logical fallacies that can branch out from these two categories, and certain types of fallacies have been used so often that people have given them names.

Fallacies are often partly accurate, which is why the human brain is tricked into thinking the entire argument is accurate and logical. This can cause problems if you are presented with false information, and the fallacy makes you believe it is true.

Fallacies are everywhere—on the internet, in relationships, in school, in politics, in advertising, and even in your own mind. This book of 50 common logical fallacies can help you identify when people are trying to trick you into believing something, or when you might unintentionally be using a fallacy yourself.

50 Common Logical Fallacies

Non Sequitur

Making a conclusion that does not logically follow from the premises.

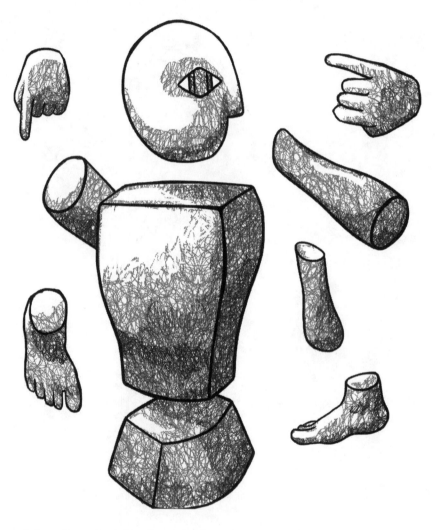

Non Sequitur is all over the place. Everything it says is disconnected nonsense, and it likes it that way. Formal fallacies look up to it as their role model.

Non Sequitur translates to "does not follow".

This fallacy appears when the arguer makes a leap in logic from the premises to the conclusion. This is invalid and compromises the form of an argument. Even if the information is accurate, it is a fallacy because the arguer draws a conclusion that has no logical support from the premises.

All formal fallacies are a type of Non Sequitur, because it is the most basic example of breaking an argument's form.

If P, then Q.
P.
Therefore X.

"I know you want fancy decorations, but listen. Chandeliers hang from the ceiling. This fan hangs from the ceiling. The fan is a chandelier."

"I saw my boyfriend having dinner with some stranger—he must be cheating on me!"

"Exercising is important for my health, and exercising outside is even better. Tomorrow is a nice day, so you need to get outside and join me in doing some exercise."

"Cars are important in today's world, especially if you have a job. I just got a new job, so you should buy me a sports car."

Non Sequitur is a sub-fallacy of...

Formal Fallacy

Gambler's Fallacy

Believing that the longer a pattern continues,
the more likely it will break or diverge.

Gambler's Fallacy enjoys messing with people. It will
manipulate probabilities and random events to make you
think that there's a trick lurking behind everything.

Gambler's Fallacy is also known as "Monte Carlo fallacy" and "fallacy of the maturity of chances".

This fallacy occurs when the arguer assumes that a certain series of unrelated events forms some sort of pattern—even though there is none—and that the pattern is more and more likely to break the longer it goes on. Gambler's Fallacy is most often seen during streaks of "bad luck" and streaks of "good luck".

The name "Monte Carlo fallacy" supposedly originates from a famous game of roulette at the Monte Carlo Casino, in which the ball landed on black 26 times in a row, causing gamblers to lose large sums of money betting against black. Gambler's Fallacy is often considered the reverse of Hot Hand Fallacy.

"If I flip a coin and get tails, the probability of getting tails on the next flip will only be 25% instead of 50%."

"I already have five daughters, so my next child will be a son."

"Lightning never strikes in the same place twice."

"I've been having bad luck lately, so things are sure to turn around."

"I know I haven't won a single thing from the lottery for years, but that just means I'll definitely win big anytime now!"

Gambler's Fallacy is a sub-fallacy of...

Formal Fallacy

Non Sequitur

Hot Hand Fallacy

Believing that the longer a pattern continues,
the less likely it will break or diverge.

Hot Hand pretends it is on your side, that your luck
is better than ever with it around. Go on, try risking
something big—things are sure to keep going well.

Hot Hand Fallacy is also known as "hot hand phenomenon" or simply "hot hand".

This fallacy, like Gambler's Fallacy, occurs when it is assumed that a certain series of unrelated events forms some sort of pattern even though there is none. However, the conclusion made about the pattern is the opposite: the longer the perceived pattern goes on, the more likely it is assumed to continue. While Gambler's Fallacy relies more on fear and suspicion, Hot Hand Fallacy relies on groundless optimism.

The term "hot hand" refers to the disproven yet popular theory that basketball players are more likely to make a successful shot if their previous shot was also successful.

"I don't need to check the weather before going out. It's been sunny all month, so today is going to be sunny as well."

"The economy just keeps getting better and better! Crashes are a thing of the past."

"I'm not usually good with gambling, but I always make a lot of money with slot machines. I have great luck with those."

"I should've stopped playing this game hours ago, but for once I've been having good luck with the randomly assigned groups for every round. Such great teammates! I can't stop now that I'm on a roll."

Hot Hand Fallacy is a sub-fallacy of...

Formal Fallacy

Non Sequitur

Masked Man Fallacy

Assuming that if one object seems to have a trait that another does not, they are different.

No one knows what Masked Man Fallacy looks like. It enjoys masquerading as one thing or another, taking advantage of any gaps in knowledge you might have.

Masked Man Fallacy is also known as "intensional fallacy", "epistemic fallacy", and "hooded man".

This fallacy makes the mistake of confusing an unverified belief with fact, then making a conclusion based on such unsound premises. A lack of certainty in the premises is what causes this argument to be invalid and fallacious.

This fallacy is based on the misuse of Leibniz's Law, which is the same concept, but with full soundness in its premises.

I think X is Z.
I think Y is not Z.
Therefore, X cannot be Y.

"I don't know who the masked man is. I know who my brother is. Therefore, my brother can't be the masked man."

"You've met Tolkien? Liar, you said you didn't know the author of 'The Silmarillion'."

"Only bad people make poor decisions. The person I'm voting for is not a bad person, so he'd never make poor decisions."

"My friends said they'd be working late today, so obviously that makes it impossible for them to have time to throw a surprise party for my birthday."

Masked Man is a sub-fallacy of...

Formal Fallacy

Non Sequitur

Affirming the Consequent

Assuming that if a claim is true, the converse
of that claim must also be true.

Affirming the Consequent likes conclusions so much that it
always puts them first. It is difficult to make heads or tails
of anything it tries to explain.

Affirming the Consequent is also known as "fallacy of the converse" and "confusion of necessity and sufficiency".

This fallacy misinterprets the initial premise by reversing it. It assumes that if the consequent of a statement (represented as Q) is true, then the antecedent (represented as P) must also be true. This reversal is known as a "converse".

This is faulty because the antecedent is not stated to be the only requirement for the consequent to be true.

If P, then Q.
Q.
Therefore, P.

"Fever is an early symptom of smallpox. I have a fever, so I must be dying of smallpox!"

"Reports show that 90% of all murders are committed by men, which means that 9 out of 10 men must actually be murderers!"

"If America's educational system was perfect, there would be a lot of American Nobel laureates. A lot of Nobel laureates are American, so the education system must indeed be perfect."

"If an important event occurred in history, then it must have been written down. This event I'm reading about must be important."

Affirming the Consequent is a sub-fallacy of...

Formal Fallacy

Non Sequitur

Denying the Antecedent

Assuming that if a claim is true, the inverse of that claim must also true.

Denying the Antecedent has backwards common sense.
It assumes that if positive things are good, then negative
things must also be good. It's only logical.

Denying the Antecedent is also known as "fallacy of the inverse".

This fallacy assumes that if the antecedent of a statement (represented as P) is false, then the consequent (represented as Q) must also be false. This reversal is known as an "inverse".

This fallacy can be avoided by inserting the phrase "if and only if" to the initial premise. Denying the Antecedent is caused by incorrect assumption that Q is the only condition in which P can exist, while in reality, P may exist under conditions other than Q.

If P, then Q.
Not P.
Therefore, not Q.

"If there's a hurricane, then there must be rain. There's no hurricane, therefore it's impossible for it to be raining."

"Dogs are animals. Humans aren't dogs, which means humans can't be animals."

"Frogs only exist in a wet environments, but there are no frogs where we're heading, so it must be too dry there."

"If you smoke or eat unhealthy foods, you'll get sick and die at an early age. I never smoke, and I eat healthy all the time, so it's impossible for me to get sick or die young."

Denying the Antecedent is a sub-fallacy of...

Formal Fallacy

Non Sequitur

Red Herring

Responding to an argument by changing the topic to something else in order to avoid it.

Red Herring does not like your topic at all. It is far too difficult to refute, so why bother? How about another topic? No, you seem good at that one. Another one then.

Red Herring is also known as *"ignoratio elenchi* (ignorance of refutation)", "missing the point", "irrelevant conclusion", and "fallacy of relevance".

This fallacy occurs when the arguer brings up a point that appears to be related to the argument but in fact is not. The new point is often an agreeable one, resulting in the illusion that the arguer wins the entire debate if the opponent agrees with it. Red Herring is often used when the arguer knows that they are in an unfavorable position and wants to avoid dealing with it. Because it is so common, there are many different Red Herring sub-fallacies.

The name "red herring" originates from the concept of using a smoked or salted herring to distract hounds with its strong smell.

"Does it really matter whether teachers should get paid more? They love teaching kids, they should be happy already!"

"I know my favorite celebrity has done some really bad things, but so have lots of others."

"I understand that you're upset at me for the huge problem I created, but I don't appreciate your tone. You're always like this when you crriticize me and I think we should focus on that instead."

"I know it's my turn to clean the house, but my birthday is coming up soon, so I should be excused this week."

Red Herring is a sub-fallacy of...

Informal
Fallacy

Special Pleading

Insisting that something is an exception to a rule or standard, without justifying why.

Special Pleading is the golden child, the exception to rules. It is special and deserves the best things of all things. Why? Well, it just does. You should accept that.

Special Pleading is also known as "overwhelming exception".

With this fallacy, the arguer acknowledges that their argument is faulty, but insists that the opponent makes an exception because their specific situation deserves it. However, it is never properly explained why the exception is warranted, so the special pleading adds nothing solid to the argument.

This fallacy may be called "failed pleading" in cases in which a reason is actually given for a potential exception, but it is faulty.

Special Pleading may be non-fallacious in cases in which the arguer does provide a reasonable explanation for why the exception should be made, thus giving credibility to the argument.

"I agree that people should be punished for their crimes, but my son is a good person who doesn't deserve this!"

"I know diet pills are usually fake or dangerous, but this next one will definitely work."

"I know you said it's a child-free wedding, but this is your niece we're talking about! She's different from all the other babies. Can't you tolerate her crying for a few hours?"

"I can't help with the yard work this week. It's dirty and difficult, and such work is beneath someone like me."

Special Pleading is a sub-fallacy of...

Informal
Fallacy

Two Wrongs Make a Right

Countering a wrongdoing with another wrongdoing to make them both appear right.

Two Wrongs Make a Right likes bad things. Two negatives cancel out to make a positive. That is how it works with math, right? Surely it works with everything else.

Two Wrongs Make a Right is sometimes known as *"tu quoque* (you as well)" in certain instances.

This fallacy occurs when an arguer sidesteps an accusation of wrongdoing by claiming that someone else did the same thing, and that should allow the arguer to do it as well. This diverts all of the negative attention onto someone else. Fairness is often a factor is this fallacy, as the arguer may insist that if someone did something wrong, then it would only be fair to let others do the same thing.

Two Wrongs Make a Right often occurs in politics and wars, and is a main driving force of "vigilante justice". The fallacy is called *"tu quoque"* when the arguer receives criticism, and attempts to negate it by throwing the same criticism back at their opponent.

"America used nuclear weapons in war, so other countries should be allowed to as well."

"You wouldn't have paid me back if I lent you money, so I'm not going to pay back what I borrowed from you."

"An eye for an eye and a tooth for a tooth."

"My opponents were cheating, so I wouldn't be doing anything wrong if I happened to cheat too."

"It's fine if I run red lights. I saw police cars doing it for no reason!"

Two Wrongs Make a Right is a sub-fallacy of...

Informal
Fallacy

Red Herring

Genetic Fallacy

Judging information based solely on where it came from, rather than what it is about.

Genetic Fallacy believes that origins are important. Even more important than what originates from those origins. We can dismiss all of that useless information.

Genetic Fallacy is also known as "fallacy of origins".

This fallacy occurs when the arguer insists that certain sources of information are end-all ideals despite being irrational, and that evidence from these sources are therefore sound. Instead of evaluating the argument based on its accuracy and logic, the arguer judges it based on how well it achieves a certain arbitrary criteria. Genetic Fallacy has many sub-fallacies which vary by the type of sources they idealize and how the arguments are used.

"Genetic" refers to origins, and the assumption that supposedly "good" sources would provide equally "good" information. The reverse is also applicable—information could be considered "bad" if the source is similarly considered "bad".

"America is always the best in what it does—it's America, after all!"

"You got that information from the internet, so it's obviously wrong. Published documents are the only source of accurate information."

"He's a terrible boss and everything he says is ridiculous. I can't believe you listen to a thing he says. Why bother? It's all complete nonsense either way."

"You know he went to a community college, right? I don't think he's the best person to talk to if you need an expert."

Genetic Fallacy is a sub-fallacy of...

Informal
Fallacy

Red Herring

Appeal to Emotion

Using a person's emotions to overrule their better judgement and logical reasoning.

Appeal to Emotions is a volatile fallacy. It appears primal and simple-minded, but with a few words, it can evoke intense reactions from within the depths of one's soul.

Appeal to Emotions is also known as *"argumentum ad passiones"*.

This fallacy prioritizes emotion over logic, using persuasive language to manipulate the feelings of others. It is very commonly seen in politics and controversial debates, and many persuasive techniques take advantage of this fallacy. Media sources often use this fallacy as well, in order to control the viewers' perception of the stories that they are reporting. The argument tactic called "loaded words" often uses Appeal to Emotion to sway listeners.

Appeal to Emotion can overlap with other fallacies due to its versatility. There are many specific types of this fallacy as well; "appeal to fear", "appeal to anger", and "appeal to empathy and compassion" are common ones.

"You should finish your food—just think of all the children in the world who are starving!"

"Of course there must be life after death. Why? Well, it would just be too sad to even consider that there might not be."

"The gunman was just a troubled teen who was going through some rough times. He used to be such a wonderful child! Please consider a lighter sentence for this poor victim of circumstance."

"Immigrants steal our jobs, commit crimes, and corrupt our culture! We must close our borders to these people!"

Appeal to Emotion is a sub-fallacy of...

Informal
Fallacy

Red Herring

Genetic
Fallacy

Etymological Fallacy

Believing that a word's current meaning must be the same as its original meaning.

Etymological Fallacy likes words and their roots. Words were always better back in the old days. "Evolution" or whatnot is just nonsense—the roots are always right.

Etymological Fallacy considers a word's original meaning to be the "real meaning" of the word, even in present-day usage. This ignores the fact that words can change meaning over time, as a normal part of the progress and evolution of language. The fallacy is often committed when the arguer realizes that a word's original meaning just happens to support their claim, and they use that to their advantage. This fallacy can often be seen when there is a generation gap between two people. An older generation may not realize or care that a word has changed meaning over time, and insist that the younger generation is using it incorrectly.

This fallacy only applies when the word's meaning has changed over time. Some words have not changed meaning at all, and so it would be accurate to claim that the meaning is the same.

"Stop saying 'bless you' when I sneeze—I told you already that I'm not religious."

"Scientists said that climate change has decimated the glaciers. Well, decimate means 1 in 10, and a 10% loss is nothing to worry about."

"So what if I said he's awful? It means he inspires awe in others—clearly it's a compliment!"

"My classmate called me a puritan because I 'look down on everyone', but that's ridiculous. 'Puritans' are English Protestants, and I'm obviously not one."

Etymological Fallacy is a sub-fallacy of...

Informal
Fallacy

Red Herring

Genetic
Fallacy

Appeal to Novelty

Believing that something is good solely because it is a recent development.

Appeal to Novelty is snobbish about old things. New things are the best, much better than those useless ancient things. Throw out all those old relics to make way for the new!

Appeal to Novelty is also known as *"argumentum ad novitatem"* and "argument of the new".

This fallacy relies on the misconception that new things are better solely because they are "novel", "state-of-the-art", and supposedly more impressive than everything that came before them. This fallacy does not take into account the fact that new things are not always perfect, or that they may be liable to fail because they have not been tested yet.

Appeal to Novelty may be non-fallacious in some situations. For example, scientific technology has improved over time, so modern-day medical practices based on evidence are typically better than older practices that were based on speculation.

"We need to get that new computer upgrade, it will be way better than our current system."

"Our current government is terrible. We need to turn things around and elect this new party, they'll make everything better!"

"That dress is so outdated. Did you see the new fashion trends for this season? You have to dress like that to look good."

"It's so great to live in a modern society! I feel bad for all those poor people living in undeveloped countries—it's sad to think that they aren't as advanced as we are."

Appeal to Novelty is a sub-fallacy of...

Informal
Fallacy

Red Herring

Genetic
Fallacy

Appeal to Authority

Assuming that an authority figure is an expert in things outside of their field of expertise.

Appeal to Authority knows better than everyone else. The authorities it mentions might be questionable, but that just means things are fine as long as you don't question them.

Appeal to Authority is also known as "false authority", "*argumentum ad verecundiam* (argument from authority)", and "misleading authority".

This fallacy occurs when the arguer uses someone in a position of authority to back their claim, even though the authority is not educated on or even related at all to the issue. People fall for Appeal to Authority because they automatically consider authority figures as good without considering whether or not the person has expertise related to the topic at hand.

When it is fallaciously assumed that the arguer is the authority on the matter, Appeal to Authority is called "*ipse dixit* (he himself said)", and is also the fallacy behind the phrase "because I said so".

"The person who was declared Woman of the Year just endorsed one of the candidates running for president, so he must be the right choice."

"I didn't believe that the moon landing was faked until a famous celebrity said it was."

"Presidents are perfect role models of honesty and integrity, just like the great President Nixon."

"My classmate said 'they' can be used as a singular pronoun, but my parents said it can only be plural. My classmate must be wrong since adults are always right."

Appeal to Authority is a sub-fallacy of...

Informal
Fallacy

Red Herring

Genetic
Fallacy

Bandwagon Fallacy

Believing that something is good because
many others believe it to be good.

Bandwagon Fallacy believes that more is better. The more
people on its side, the more right it feels. Look at how
happy everyone is. Come and jump on the bandwagon.

Bandwagon Fallacy is also known as *"argumentum ad populum (appeal to the people)"*, "appeal to popularity", "argument by consensus", and "appeal to majority".

This fallacy considers popularity to be the best way to judge the truth of something. While it is possible for something to be both correct and popular, there is no inherent link between the two. Peer pressure is often a factor in this fallacy.

Information that gets attention is more likely to be considered accurate, because if something was wrong with it, someone would presumably have noticed and pointed it out. However, it is possible that some people had indeed noticed and tried to bring attention to it, but they were not able to change popular opinion.

"This new diet sounds ridiculous, but a lot of my friends are trying it, so it must be good."

"We're only hiring popular actors for the lead role in this movie. Since they are popular, the movie is guaranteed to be successful."

"Our product is the number one choice—everyone loves it, and we know that you will too!"

"The idea proposed at the meeting appears to be innovative and well thought out, but it was rejected by almost everyone in the group. There must be something wrong with it.

Bandwagon Fallacy is a sub-fallacy of...

Informal
Fallacy

Red Herring

Genetic
Fallacy

Appeal to Tradition

Believing something is good because it has been around for a long time.

Appeal to Tradition is a self-sustaining fallacy. The older side writes the rules, and though the younger side is not sure where the rules came from, it follows them anyway.

Appeal to Tradition is also known as *"argumentum ad antiquitatem"*, "traditional wisdom", "appeal to common practice", and "appeal to antiquity".

This fallacy relies on the misconception that old things are better solely because they have "stood the test of time" or were created by "elders" and thus figures of authority. This fallacy does not take into account that people in the past may have been wrong or made mistakes when they created or supported something.

This fallacy is often associated with Naturalistic Fallacy and Appeal to Authority. The opposite of Appeal to Tradition is called Appeal to Novelty, which uses a similar concept but instead considers new, novel ideas to be the ideal, rather than old, traditional ones.

"You bring up excellent points, but we can't just change our code of conduct. We've been following it for decades."

"Drones are just a fad. The postal service has always been around, and it always will be."

"This is how it's always been done."

"Technology is ruining society. Back in the old days, people used to talk to their friends! Now, they're glued to their computers and phones, going on Facebook, texting and calling people. No social interaction at all!"

Appeal to Tradition is a sub-fallacy of...

Informal
Fallacy

Red Herring

Genetic
Fallacy

Straw Man

Misinterpreting an opponent's argument in a way that makes it easier to attack or condemn.

Straw Man always talks about how scary its opponents are, and the awful things they do. But not to worry, Straw Man will defeat them all before you can even see for yourself.

Straw Man is also known as "Aunt Sally" in the UK.

This fallacy occurs when the arguer takes an opponent's argument and subtly changes it to a different argument that is easier to condemn and attack. Defeating this distorted "argument" creates the illusion that the actual argument is defeated. It is a diversionary tactic that results in both vilifying the opponent and winning the debate. Straw Man can be accidental; this often happens when the arguer jumps to conclusions and misunderstands the opponent's argument to be something that it is not.

Straw Man is named after the concept of building a dummy out of straw, attacking and defeating it, and then declaring victory as if it was a strong opponent.

"My brother didn't like Romeo and Juliet—I can't believe he has such disdain for classic literature!"

"What do you mean I can't take a month-long vacation? So you're saying I'm never allowed to relax and have fun, huh?"

"My employees think I should raise their wages because I pay them too little. I can't believe how greedy they are!"

"My opponent says that he wants to build more schools around the nation. Are you just going to sit there while he steals your hard-earned money to fund his pet projects?"

Straw Man is a sub-fallacy of...

Informal
Fallacy

Red Herring

Genetic
Fallacy

Ad Hominem

Attacking the character or traits of the opponent instead of addressing the argument.

Ad Hominem is armed with a multitude of weapons to tear apart its opponents. It could care less about any arguments you try to make, only about winning and beating you.

Ad Hominem is also known as *"argumentum ad hominem* (argument towards person)," "character assassination", and "personal attack".

This fallacy is used to distract the audience from the argument at hand by redirecting their attention to unrelated negative traits of the opponent. This causes the opponent to look bad even if the argument they make is logical. This is an extremely common fallacy, and is considered unprofessional in formal settings. Prejudice is a common factor in Ad Hominem, with arguers often making use of stereotypes of a group their opponent belongs to.

If the personal attack is relevant to the claims, it may not be fallacious. For example, one could question the trustworthiness of someone who frequently lies.

"How can you expect people to take you seriously if you can't even speak English well?"

"This news reporter wore the same jacket last week—that's so unsightly and unprofessional, she should be replaced by someone else!"

"You shouldn't give that person the job—he's a former criminal; you don't know what he'll do next."

"His workplace is always messy, and he always looks so unkempt. His brain is probably the same way, I don't think he will make a good research partner."

Ad Hominem is a sub-fallacy of...

Informal
Fallacy

Red Herring

Genetic
Fallacy

Ad Iram

Trying to undermine an opponent's authority
by accusing them of being angry.

Anger is bad. Ad Iram is out searching for angry people to
attack. If the search proves too difficult, it only needs to
pretend the opponent is angry and attack them anyway.

Ad Iram is Latin for "to anger".

This fallacy occurs when the arguer accuses their opponent of being angry, or of having an argument that is rooted in anger, even when there may be no indication of such a thing. Anger is often associated with irrationality, and the implication is that the opponent's arguments are baseless if made from anger. Since it is easier to assign guilt to something as abstract as emotions than it is to deny it, Ad Iram is a popular tactic.

Ad Iram is a sub-fallacy of both Ad Hominem and Straw Man because it forces a misrepresentation onto the opponent that causes them to look bad, then attacks that misrepresentation because it is easier to "defeat".

"You think people in poverty are being mistreated because you're poor yourself! You're just sore about your own situation."

"You're just being emotional now. It's probably that time of the month, huh?"

"You're blaming other people for problems that are your own fault. All of that pent-up rage is clouding your judgement!"

"You're accusing me of things again? You're being unreasonable! Why don't you calm down and maybe we can talk about this once your tantrum is done?"

Ad Iram is a sub-fallacy of...

Red Herring   Genetic Fallacy   Ad Hominem   Straw Man

Moving the Goalposts

Continually changing the criteria or "goal" that the opponent must meet.

Moving the Goalposts takes the form of an enchanting spectre. It leads people onwards, promising a goal just ahead, but stays out of reach and never stops moving.

Moving the Goalposts is also known as "raising the bar" and "shifting sands".

This fallacy happens often as a result of underestimating the opponent's ability to reach an initial goal set for them. In response, the arguer sets a new goal in hopes that it cannot be reached. This fallacy is often used to shift the "burden of proof". Although the goals can be changed to anything with this fallacy, it is most commonly changed to something more difficult to achieve. "Raising the bar" specifically refers to this type of change.

The term "moving the goalposts" originates from sports such as American football, in which people would move the goalposts in order to make it more difficult for the opposing team to score.

"Sure, you can make the goal if it's half a field away, but what about an entire field away?"

"I won't admit you're right until you show me proof. It probably won't even be real proof though...People can fake anything these days."

"You've always done an excellent job here, but you need to work overtime and bring in more profits to our company if you really want to get a raise."

"I know I said I was hungry and didn't care at all where we went, but I hate pizza! You should've chosen something other than pizza."

Moving the Goalposts is a sub-fallacy of...

Informal
Fallacy

Red Herring

Ambiguity Fallacy

Using ambiguous language to support an
argument and hide any flaws.

Ambiguity Fallacy always keeps itself hidden, showing only
hints of itself. It lets people make their own conclusions
about its looks, but its real appearance remains a mystery.

Ambiguity Fallacy is also known simply as "vagueness".

This fallacy uses premises that are unclear and impossible to draw a proper conclusion from. This is often due to vague grammar, but can also refer to when an arguer explains ideas and concepts vaguely. The intention of this fallacy is to give the impression that a faulty premise is actually solid. The arguer may realize that their argument has holes in its logic, but instead of improving or verifying the argument, they may use this fallacy to mask its flaws.

There are many different types of Ambiguity Fallacy, depending on what parts of the premise are ambiguous. Equivocation is one of its most well-known sub-fallacies but Quote Mining is also a common sight.

"I have the right to free speech, and that means it's right for me to verbally threaten people if I choose to."

"My boss told me 'have a good day' earlier this morning, so I left work to go have a good day."

"Gay people should be allowed to have civil unions and the same rights as straight couples, but they shouldn't be allowed to marry."

"Learning logic and fallacies helps people form better arguments. But arguments are bad, they cause people to get angry at each other. We should avoid learning how to argue. That's how to achieve peace!"

Fallacy of Ambiguity is a sub-fallacy of...

Informal
Fallacy

Quote Mining

Quoting someone's words in a way that
changes their original meaning.

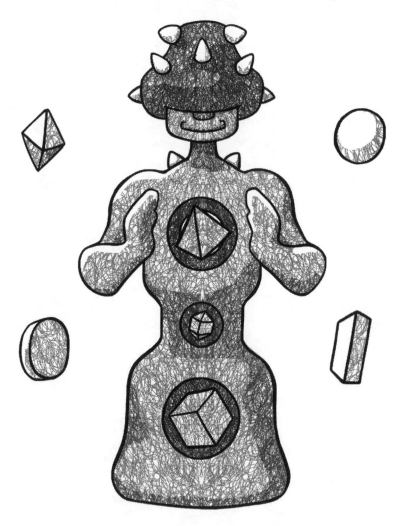

Quote Mining is a mix-and-match-er. It likes to cut parts
out, and maybe add on some words too. If the meaning
happens to change in the process, that just makes it better.

Quote Mining is also known as "fallacy of quoting out of context" and "contextomy".

This fallacy uses a quote as evidence to back a claim, but neglects to mention the context of the quote's origin. This changes the actual meaning of the quote to better suit the arguers claim.

While Quote Mining is often used intentionally, it can also occur by accident if the arguer misinterprets someone's words, or if they themselves only know of the quote outside of its original context due to a lack of thorough research.

This fallacy often overlaps with other fallacies, such as an Appeal to Authority caused by misquoting an authoritative figure.

"If I may be so bold as to quote Hamlet, Act III, Scene iii, Line 87: 'No'."

"New York Times calls it 'an excellent book' [if you want to waste a perfectly good afternoon on such a terrible read]."

"Curiosity killed the cat [but satisfaction brought it back]."

"Great minds think alike [but fools rarely differ]."

"As Carl Schurz declared in 1872, 'My country, right or wrong; [if right, to be kept right; and if wrong, to be set right].'"

Quote Mining is a sub-fallacy of...

Informal
Fallacy

Fallacy of
Ambiguity

Equivocation

Using a multi-layered concept vaguely so the meaning can be changed to suit the argument.

Equivocation divides itself into pieces that look the same yet not quite. They like to switch places with each other to trick people into thinking there is only one of them.

Equivocation is also known as "doublespeak".

This fallacy typically uses a single word that has multiple definitions, and manipulates it to mean more than one thing through the course of the argument. The result is an argument that appears to make sense on the surface but is actually nonsensical if one examines each word closely. Equivocation is commonly used in jokes and riddles but can be seen in actual arguments as well. This fallacy often occurs when the arguer is unaware of, or rejects, another definition of a word or subject.

Equivocation usually involves manipulating homonyms to mean different things, but can also refer to the concept of treating two ideas or subjects as the same even though they are separate.

"Don't you know that two wrongs don't make a right, but three lefts do?"

"My teacher said that knowledge is power, but power leads to corruption, so I'm better off not learning."

"I was told that if I graduate from law school, I can get a good job. Now that I've graduated, I can get a good job as a rocket scientist."

"You're a feminist? So that means you hate men, right?"

"A sandwich is bread with content inside, so a hot dog is a sandwich."

Equivocation is a sub-fallacy of...

Informal
Fallacy

Fallacy of
Ambiguity

Fallacy of the Grey

Assuming that two things are the same if they share a distant or vague similarity.

Fallacy of the Grey tends to spend its time not caring about things. People are so divisive. Why bother separating things when they can all just be one big mess?

Fallacy of the Grey is also known as "continuum fallacy", "sorites fallacy", "bald man fallacy", and "fallacy of the heap".

This fallacy occurs when the arguer assumes that there is no "black or white" to a complex issue, and it is instead made up of shades of grey. The assumption that follows is that all shades of grey are the same, and thus there is no difference between the two positions. This disregards the fact that "grey" can be very light or very dark, and not just one indistinguishable shade.

Fallacy of the Grey functions by using increments ambiguously, relying on the fact that there may be no defined line or cut-off point that clearly separates one subject from another. As such, it plays off of the traits of Equivocation.

"Assault and murder are both crimes, so both offenders should be given the same punishment."

"I always play the penny machine at the casino. That way, I can play as many times as I want and never lose much money."

"If I lose one hair, I won't go bald, nor will I go bald after losing another, thus it's impossible for me to go bald no matter how much hair I lose."

"A heap of sand is still a heap if I take one grain out. It remains a heap no matter how much I take out."

Fallacy of the Grey is a sub-fallacy of...

Informal Fallacy

Fallacy of Ambiguity

Equivocation

Inflation of Conflict

Believing that if two or more expert sources disagree on a matter, none of them are right.

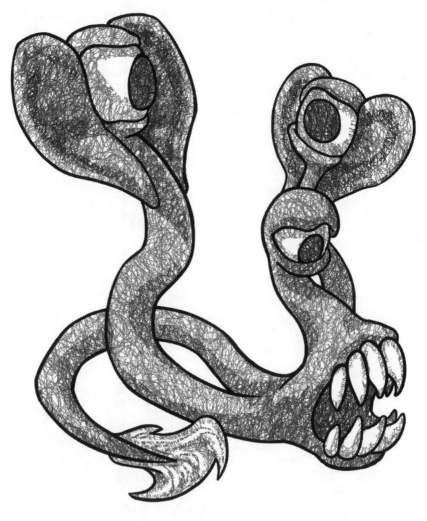

Inflation of Conflict is always arguing with itself. It usually ends up ignoring the entire issue and doing whatever it wants, though that gets itself lost more often than not.

Inflation of Conflict occurs when the arguer assumes that if there is no consensus on a topic, even among experts in the field, then it must be the case that everyone is wrong and no one knows anything. This is a faulty assumption, because it is possible that one expert is correct or close to the truth, while others may be completely wrong.

Inflation of Conflict can be used as a way to suggest that because there is so much disagreement, it would be reasonable to accept an amateur theory as holding the same credibility as expert ones.

Since Inflation of Conflict disregards any vaguely uncertain positions under the assumption that they are all the same, the fallacy is a specific type of Fallacy of the Grey.

"All of the books I've read say different things on how to raise children. I'll just stop taking advice and raise them however I want."

"No one can agree on whether or not Bigfoot exists, so the truth is a complete mystery."

"Experts are still debating over whether Mars or Europa would be better to sustain life, so we should consider my suggestion that Mercury is just as likely to work."

"Why should we even have a President if the candidates disagree on everything? We should just give up on the idea of a unified country."

Inflation of Conflict is a sub-fallacy of...

Informal
Fallacy

Fallacy of
Ambiguity

Equivocation

Fallacy of the
Grey

Naturalistic Fallacy

Describing something with positive or
negative words that lack specific meanings.

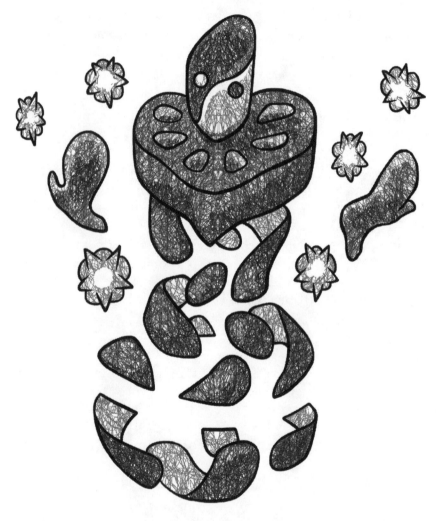

Naturalistic Fallacy is a little vague. It might be missing
some key details here and there, but it insists that nothing is
wrong, everything is fine, everything is great.

Naturalistic Fallacy is also known as "is-ought fallacy".

This fallacy uses vague adjectives to imply that something is good or bad without explaining why exactly they are. The term "natural" here means "how things should be". Naturalistic Fallacy assumes that good things are already happening, and that bad things are not happening at all, thus people should keep things the same as always in order to maintain the status quo.

Naturalistic Fallacy's other name, "is-ought fallacy" refers to the concept that if something "is" the case, it is presumably good, and therefore it "ought" to, or should be, the case. Similarly, if something "is not" the case, then it is bad and therefore it "ought not" be the case.

"War and murder are just part of human nature. It's just how things are. It's impossible for humans to be peaceful creatures."

"Smoking can't be all that bad for you. If it was, it'd be illegal."

"If you're a woman, you have to have kids. That's what women were created to do."

"Why should we need to look into pay gap issues in America? The Equal Pay Act was signed into law ages ago, so it's impossible for sexism to exist."

Naturalistic Fallacy is a sub-fallacy of...

Informal
Fallacy

Fallacy of
Ambiguity

Equivocation

Appeal to Nature

Believing that something is good because it is natural, or bad because it is unnatural.

Appeal to Nature uses its beauty and elegance to attract its unwitting victims. It ensnares them with its natural teeth, natural spikes, and natural inclination to consume people.

Appeal to Nature is also known as *"argumentum ad naturam"*.

This fallacy considers "nature" to be the best way to judge something, evaluating the worth or quality of something based solely on how natural it is. This causes problems partially because the concept of "nature" itself is vague and difficult to define. Due to the importance placed on this single aspect, attempts made by the opponent to criticize the subject using any other criteria are ignored. This fallacy is commonly seen in advertisements boasting "organic" or "all-natural" products.

Appeal to Nature and Naturalistic Fallacy are often confused due to their similar names and concepts. Appeal to Nature is a more specific sub-fallacy of Naturalistic Fallacy.

"This medicine can't be found in nature, therefore it is bad for us."

"We should not select that candidate for the position—his work history is good, but his tattoos are unprofessional."

"This organization is using high-yielding GMOs to feed starving people. Since GMOs are not natural, we need to shut them down."

"Technological inventions messed with the natural order of life. Society is degenerating because we have things like computers, cell phones, and the internet."

Appeal to Nature is a sub-fallacy of...

Informal
Fallacy

Fallacy of
Ambiguity

Equivocation

Naturalistic
Fallacy

Just-World Fallacy

Assuming that anything that happens to someone happens because they deserve it.

Just-World Fallacy insists that the world must have justice, natural or not. If it sees a situation that is unjust, then surely something out there must set it right...

Just-World Fallacy is also known as "just-world hypothesis".

This fallacy is based on the assumption that the world is fair and just, and that anything good or bad that happens must be because the person had it coming to them. People often have trouble accepting that injustices occur in life, and try to rationalize them with the concept of karma. Though Just-World Fallacy can apply to good occurrences, negative occurrences are often more problematic because they may lead to victim-blaming.

This fallacy can be seen aimed at the arguer's own actions as well, such as in the assumption that doing good things means that only good things will come their way. This often leads to anger or discontentment if bad things happen instead.

"He got what was coming to him."

"I think you should give your lottery winnings to me. I work hard, volunteer, give to the community, and deserve it. You don't do any of that, so naturally you don't deserve anything."

"Your daughter is only getting bullied because she doesn't fit in. The bullies aren't doing anything wrong, your daughter is the problem."

"My neighbor accidentally left his doors unlocked yesterday, so it's his own fault that he ended up getting robbed. The robbers shouldn't be punished, they were only doing what's expected of them."

Just-World Fallacy is a sub-fallacy of...

Informal Fallacy

Fallacy of Ambiguity

Equivocation

Naturalistic Fallacy

Argumentum ad Nauseum

Repeating an argument over and over until it feels like it is common sense or truth.

Argumentum ad Nauseam is often told that it tends to overdo things. But hey, whatever works. You can hit anything as long as you fire at it enough times, right?

Argumentum ad Nauseum is also known as "argument to the point of disgust" and "fallacy of repetition".

This fallacy relies on claims that have been stated so often that people begin to accept them as a simple matter of truth rather than a potential point to criticize. This can be seen through the spread of misinformation, often by word of mouth or on the internet, and through commercials that repeat information or phrases with the intent of making the information stick in the viewer's brain.

Argumentum ad Nauseam sometimes overlaps with other fallacies, such as Quote Mining, in which a quote is repeated over and over until everyone believes it, regardless of whether it is true or not.

"Frankenstein isn't a doctor, he's the monster that the doctor created! Just look in any Halloween store and you'll see that I'm right."

"The Loch Ness monster is real! This many people wouldn't know about it if it was a hoax."

"Remember kids, if someone offers you drugs, 'just say no'!"

"What do you mean cats are lactose-intolerant? I don't believe you. Everyone knows cats love milk."

"Marie Antoinette was killed because she said 'Let them eat cake'."

Argumentum ad Nauseam is a sub-fallacy of...

Informal
Fallacy

Argument to Moderation

Assuming that a compromise between two sides must be the best choice.

Argument to Moderation does not have a mind for minor details. If it cannot decide between one thing or another, it will decide that the exact middle is the right choice.

Argument to Moderation is also known as "*argumentum ad temperantiam*", "middle ground", and "golden mean fallacy".

This fallacy neglects to consider either side of an issue, instead favoring the concept of a "compromise". While it is possible for good results to come from a compromise, this fallacy assumes that both sides are equally accurate, even though it may be the case that one person is right and the other is wrong. Even in the case that both sides are equally in the right, the middle ground between the two is not always the best solution.

Argument to Moderation is often considered the opposite of False Dilemma, because it presents one moderate solution rather than two extreme ones.

"You say this purse is worth $50, and I think it's worth nothing, so it's only fair that you sell it to me for $25."

"My teacher says the earth is round, but my little sister says it's flat. It must actually be an oval."

"Our favorite TV dramas are airing at the same time, so I will watch the first half of my show, and you can watch the last half of yours."

"The abolitionists wanted to outlaw slavery in America, and the pro-slavery factions wanted to keep it. Therefore, it was right of them to compromise with some free states and some slave states."

Argument to Moderation is a sub-fallacy of...

Informal
Fallacy

Sunk-Cost Fallacy

Refusing to cut losses in a worsening situation
because it feels like it would be a waste.

Sunk-Cost Fallacy is summoned by failed ventures and lost
investments. With so much at risk, why not dive down and
try to get it all back? It will be waiting for you.

Sunk-Cost Fallacy is also known as "Concorde fallacy", "escalation bias", and "commitment effect".

This fallacy occurs when someone has lost time, effort, or money due a poor decision or situation, but thinks that as long as they continue investing in it, they can somehow get it back. "Sunk cost" is a term in economics that refers to a cost that has already been lost and cannot be recovered. This fallacy can be seen in everyday life, particularly in financial matters such as business or gambling.

Sunk-Cost Fallacy's other name, "Concorde fallacy", is a reference to Concorde, a supersonic passenger jet that was costly to maintain from the very start, but was kept operating despite financial losses for three decades before it was finally retired.

"I can't just stop playing poker after this kind of loss! I can definitely win it back if I keep trying."

"I don't like taking French classes anymore, but I've already taken two years of it, so I might as well continue."

"I decided to make my own Halloween costume this year, but it's not turning out right. I've already bought the materials though, so I'll just have to make do."

"I know things are looking bad, but we already spent thousands of dollars on this project. We can't give up or it'll all be for nothing!"

Sunk-Cost Fallacy is a sub-fallacy of...

Informal
Fallacy

Faulty Generalization

Making a general claim based on a small amount of information.

Faulty Generalization likes umbrella terms and jumping to conclusions. It likes to push the limits and see what can be made with just the tiniest amount of knowledge.

Faulty Generalization is also known as "overgeneralization", "hasty generalization", and "unrepresentative sample".

This fallacy occurs when an arguer has a limited view or understanding of a subject, and uses what little information they have to make an incorrect statement about the matter as a whole. Faulty Generalization is often what occurs when it feels like the arguer is "jumping to conclusions". Complex topics such as race and religion are often plagued by this fallacy due to a lack of understanding among many people.

Faulty Generalization is a very common informal logical fallacy, and has many sub-fallacies that branch off from it, such as Faulty Analogy and Slippery Slope.

"Everyone in my book club has brown hair—there must be a link between people with brown hair and liking books!"

"My dog is friendly and likes people. Dogs make the best pets."

"You're eating a doughnut for lunch today? I didn't know you had such an unhealthy lifestyle, you're going to get fat! Why don't you try a salad instead?"

"I spent a few minutes searching online for proof of your argument but couldn't find any. You must be lying."

Faulty Generalization is a sub-fallacy of...

Informal
Fallacy

Toupée Fallacy

Assuming that something is always the case because exceptions are harder to notice.

Toupée Fallacy stands out, but only when it wants to. It evades attention most of the time, preferring instead to slink around in the shadows unnoticed.

Toupée Fallacy is named after the assumption that all toupées look fake because the arguer has never seen one that they could not tell was fake. This overlooks the fact that if a toupée looked real, the arguer would not have noticed it was a toupée in the first place. The same concept applies to anything that receives attention only in certain situations, causing people to assume that the attention-garnering aspect is an accurate representation of the entire subject. Since this fallacy makes a general statement based on a limited amount of information, it is a type of Faulty Generalization.

Toupée Fallacy is called "spotlight fallacy" when it applies to media attention. It is often assumed that events reported by the media are a true representation of reality as a whole, when in fact it only covers a limited type or amount of information.

"My city has zero confirmed counts of unreported crimes. It's a safe place to live."

"Asians are really easy to recognize, I can tell with just a glance. I've never seen an Asian person who I'd mistake as Caucasian."

"Transgender people are all so obvious to spot, I've never met a transgender person who wasn't blatantly transgender."

"Mentally ill people are all violent criminals! Every time the news mentions them, they're always doing something terrible. We should lock them up so everyone is safe."

Toupée Fallacy is a sub-fallacy of...

Informal
Fallacy

Faulty
Generalization

Slippery Slope

Insisting that a situation will lead to a chain of events that have an exaggerated outcome.

Slippery Slope changes in consistency, shifting between solid and unstable at will. It has a habit of jumping to conclusions that suit it, then pretending it is the truth.

Slippery Slope is also known as "domino effect", "camel's nose", and "argument of the beard".

This fallacy appears when the arguer avoids addressing the opponent's original argument by making up fake or exaggerated consequences of that argument, and attacking them instead. Because the consequences are more clearly understood to be negative, it tricks others into agreeing with the arguer rather than questioning whether or not the consequences would realistically happen in the first place.

Slippery Slope is not necessarily fallacious. If the suggested sequence of events is logical and valid, then it is a reasonable argument and not a fallacy.

"If you vote for my opponent, he'll turn this country into a dictatorship, wars will start, and our nation will become a dystopia!"

"You shouldn't go on the internet. You'll never make friends in real life if you become a shut-in."

"I have nothing against the idea of you hanging out with friends, but it opens the door to terrible things like delinquency and crime."

"If you learn a new language, you'll start forgetting your first language. Soon you won't be able to communicate or get a job, and then you'll be homeless! Learning new languages is a terrible idea."

Slippery Slope is a sub-fallacy of...

Informal
Fallacy

Faulty
Generalization

Questionable Cause

Assuming that one event must have caused another, even if there is no basis for it.

Questionable Cause was supposed to be two different creatures, but they fused into one and can no longer separate. They have turned into something else now.

Questionable Cause is also known as "*non causa pro causa* (non-cause for cause)", "false cause", and "causal fallacy".

This fallacy occurs when the arguer incorrectly assumes the cause of something, based on faulty reasoning. It often occurs when the arguer jumps to conclusions after perceiving what looks like a pattern between two or more events, when in reality there is no link at all.

One of the most common versions of this fallacy is "correlation implies causation (*cum hoc, ergo propter hoc*)": if two things happen at the same time, it is assumed that one must have caused the other. If one thing happens after another and it is assumed that the former caused the latter, it is called "*post hoc, ergo propter hoc*".

"I passed all of my final exams after buying this good luck charm. It looks like these things really do work!"

"It's hot whenever the sun is out, which means the hot weather must summon the sun."

"Piracy has declined, while at the same time, global warming has gotten worse. The lack of pirates is causing global warming!"

"Technology has improved tremendously lately and more people are undergoing surgeries these days. Technology is causing people to be less healthy than they were in the old days."

Questionable Cause is a sub-fallacy of...

Informal
Fallacy

Faulty
Generalization

Tokenism

Making a token effort to look admirable, but not following through past that.

Tokenism likes being praised, but also likes doing nothing. It spends its time hiding behind its surface camouflage to trick people into thinking it is nicer than it actually is.

Tokenism occurs when an attempt is made to achieve some kind of ethically appealing goal, such as social equality, but the attempt does not move past the first step. This "token effort" is often made to be a substitution of the bigger goal, and gives the illusion that it evens the scales and no further work has to be done. This can also be seen in attempts to counter accusations of inequality, such as naming one or two original female superheroes to dismiss the argument that there are far more male ones.

This fallacy is commonly seen when trying to achieve equality with minorities. People belonging to a majority may be used to rarely seeing minorities in their field. They might think that hiring one diverse employee is such a big move that they consider their goal achieved with that inclusion alone.

"I'm not racist, I have a black friend!"

"I used to think that billionaire celebrity was greedy and self-centered, but he just donated $1000 to charity, so I must have been all wrong about him."

"All of the scientists we hired are men—we need more gender equality in the workplace. We should bring one or two women on staff, that'll even things out."

"There's so much diversity in films these days. An Asian actress was even nominated for an Academy Award just last year!"

ᚖokenism is a sub-fallacy of...

Informal
Fallacy

Faulty
Generalization

Fallacy of Composition

Claiming that if part of something has a certain trait, the entire thing has that trait.

Fallacy of Composition knows that the heart is made of muscles, veins, and arteries. Hearts are an important part of people, so it figures people must be just like hearts.

Fallacy of Composition is often grouped together with Fallacy of Division, and the two are also collectively known as "fallacy of composition and division", "category error", "category mistake", and "distributive fallacy".

This fallacy occurs when the subject is part of a group of things, or a "whole", and it is assumed that whatever traits the subject has, the group must have them as well. It is often seen in stereotypes when applied to people or cultures.

Fallacy of Composition can be differentiated from its "sibling", Fallacy of Division, by remembering that the subject the fallacy is referring to is the smaller parts that make up the "composition" of the whole group.

"My old bike got new tires, so now it's new!"

"The girl I dated said she liked guys with muscles, but then another girl I met said she didn't care for them at all. Girls are so indecisive, they need to stop changing their minds!"

"Pennies are worth one cent, so if I gather one hundred pennies, I'll have an entire pile that's worth one cent."

"I don't understand why everyone says Facebook has so much drama. Everyone in my Facebook group is really nice and welcoming. It makes no sense."

Fallacy of Composition is a sub-fallacy of...

Informal
Fallacy

Faulty
Generaliztion

Fallacy of Division

Claiming that if something has a certain trait, parts of that thing must have the same trait.

Fallacy of Division knows that people are living creatures, and organs are parts of people, so it figures that organs must surely be living creatures as well.

Fallacy of Division is often grouped together with Fallacy of Composition, and the two are also collectively known as "fallacy of composition and division", "category error", "category mistake", and "distributive fallacy".

This fallacy occurs when the subject is a group of things, or a "whole", and it is assumed that whatever traits the whole group in general has, the "parts" that are inside of the group must have them as well.

Fallacy of Division can be differentiated from its "sibling", Fallacy of Composition, by remembering that the subject is the whole group, and the fallacy is trying to "divide" the whole group into smaller versions of itself.

"I wholeheartedly support my political party, and I will support any candidate from that party."

"You can't love your country but at the same time criticize how it's run! Either you love all of it or you don't."

"This dollar bill is worth one dollar, so if I tear it into four pieces, I'll have four dollars."

"You said you like guys, and I'm a guy, so that means you like me!"

"A skull is made of separate bones, which must also be called skulls."

Fallacy of Division is a sub-fallacy of...

Informal
Fallacy

Faulty
Generaliztion

Faulty Analogy

Comparing one subject to an unrelated one in order to change the impression of the former.

Faulty Analogy can change itself to look like anything. An analogy can be whatever you want it to be, but maybe some of them are not as great as they sounded in your head.

Faulty Analogy occurs when the arguer tries to compare one subject to another in order to prove a point, but fails due to the lack of actual similarities between the two. Analogies are commonly used in everyday life because they help people make decisions or understand the world around them better. People often use the same methods to explain arguments, hoping that it helps their cause, but it may end up being a Faulty Analogy. Depending on the arguer's intentions, this fallacy could occur intentionally or by accident.

Although analogies can be very useful to help explain an argument, it is important to make sure that the analogy is sound and the two subjects actually do share the same concept, rather than a vague similarity or something forced.

"Of course I can take care of children. I've taken care of dogs and hamsters before."

"If women want to be allowed to take their shirts off in public, then men should be allowed to take their pants off in public."

"You shouldn't go to college if you don't have enough money for it, just like you shouldn't buy an expensive car that you can't afford."

"You can't charge me with a felony just because I used a fake ID to sneak into a government building. Teenagers use fake IDs to buy alcohol all the time—it'd be ridiculous to charge them with a felony!"

Faulty Analogy is a sub-fallacy of...

Informal
Fallacy

Faulty
Generaliztion

Association Fallacy

Comparing one subject to an unrelated one in order to transfer its connotation.

Association Fallacy is extreme in everything it thinks and feels. It will glorify anything it loves, and anything it hates will be dragged through the dirt without mercy.

Association Fallacy occurs when the arguer tries to force a certain overtone onto their subject in order to avoid having to use logic to do so. The arguer makes an analogy between their subject and something that has a clear connotation, usually positive or negative; this association makes the subject look either better or worse. The goal of this fallacy is to transfer a connotation from an unrelated subject to the arguer's subject. This connotation would then act as "proof" that the arguer is right because the connotation of the first subject is clear and widely agreed upon, while the irrationality of its transferal stays largely unnoticed.

The positive version of Association Fallacy is called "honor by association", while the negative version is called "guilt by association". The latter is often a type of Ad Hominem.

"We need to hire a beautiful woman to sell our product—a great salesgirl makes products great."

"Electric cars are good for the environment. If you don't drive one, you must be in denial about the reality of climate change."

"I know you all love the former President, and I think he's great too! I agree with a lot of things he did, and that's why you should vote for me. I'd be just as great a President as he was."

"My old roommate was a vegan, and she was so rude to anyone who wasn't a vegan. Vegans are all such intolerant people."

Association Fallacy is a sub-fallacy of...

Informal
Fallacy

Faulty
Generalization

Faulty Analogy

Oversimplification

Assuming that a complex issue is much simpler than it actually is.

Oversimplification tends to jump to conclusions a lot.
Surely a simple problem must have a simple solution. Life
is not so complicated that it would require thinking.

Oversimplification, as its name suggests, occurs when the arguer oversimplifies a situation and disregards any complexities involved with it. As such, the arguer often suggests a simple solution to fix what they might see as a straightforward problem. This can cause communication issues between the arguer and their opponent because there is a discrepancy between how they see the same issue. Oversimplification is often caused by not understanding the complexities of multi-layer topics. It is a common mistake made by people who have just started learning about a topic, and can be remedied with more research.

This fallacy is called "causal oversimplification" when the arguer assumes there is one single cause that contributes to an event, when in reality there may be more.

"You're working minimum wage and your boss is underpaying you? You should just hire a lawyer and sue him!"

"All it'll take to stop illegal immigration is building a wall around our borders."

"If people are stuck in poverty, it means they're just not working hard enough or are spending too much on frivolous things."

"I think that both Presidential candidates are bad, so the best choice is to not vote at all. That's the best way to send the message that I want better options!"

Oversimplification is a sub-fallacy of...

Informal
Fallacy

Faulty
Generalization

Fallacy of Equity

Treating people or things as equal, regardless
of inherent or initial inequality.

Fallacy of Equity knows the secret to equality. It treats
everything the same because the world is perfect already,
and all it needs to do is make things more perfect.

Fallacy of Equity is also known as "color blindness" when used in cases of race.

This fallacy uses a excessive form of equality which tricks people into believing that an argument is good and virtuous even when it is not. It assumes that people are all exactly the same in all aspects of their lives, and thus no one requires different treatment. Equal treatment appears to be fair, but it may disregard or erase the concept of individuality in the process.

Fallacy of Equity often occurs with good intentions, in that the arguer wants to treat everyone equally, but the incorrect assumption that people are already on equal ground instead allows inequality to continue.

"Able-bodied people should be allowed to use handicap parking spaces if they feel like it."

"I was passing out cake to the children, but I noticed one of them had already taken a slice. I gave him another one anyway to be fair."

"The five-year-old and fifteen-year-old will both be running the same distance in order to ensure a fair race."

"I don't care if you're black, white, green or purple! We all have the same experiences, same pasts, and same lives, and that's why we shouldn't pass any laws that are exclusive to any one certain race."

Fallacy of Equity is a sub-fallacy of...

Informal
Fallacy

Faulty
Generalization

Over-
simplification

Cherry Picking

Choosing evidence that supports your argument while ignoring evidence against it.

Cherry Picking lurks in bad sources as you research. It is harmless when made of good cherries, but when the bad ones pile up, things might start looking bad for you.

Cherry Picking is also known as "suppressed evidence", "fallacy of incomplete evidence", "half-truth fallacy", and "one-sidedness".

Though this fallacy is seen in arguments, it begins manifesting in the information-gathering stage of research. Due to bias, the arguer only picks sources that support their claims while rejecting anything that disproves them, regardless of how good the sources are. Anyone can publish anything on the internet and in the media, as well as through more traditional sources like books or written documents, so it is important to check that sources are credible.

This fallacy is named after the actual task of picking cherries; the aim is to pick only the cherries that look good to you, while throwing out any that you find to be unpleasant.

"Get a free TV by entering our sweepstakes!* (*Only paying members can enter.)"

"I don't care how many sources you say you have—this source that I found supports my side, and that proves I'm right."

"I got fired from my old job because I slacked off instead of working, but I'll just tell my new employers that I 'left' my old job after some 'creative differences'."

"Many scientists agree that this treatment can cure any illness. And by 'many', I mean more than one."

Cherry Picking is a sub-fallacy of...

Informal
Fallacy

Anecdotal Fallacy

Basing an argument on one's own personal experience rather than factual information.

Anecdotal Evidence loves and admires everything about itself, ignoring anything else it sees. It is not very in touch with reality, but then again, it prefers life that way.

Anecdotal Fallacy is also known as "misleading vividness" and "fallacy of anecdotal evidence".

This fallacy considers one's own experience to be a sound information source, not considering that one's life can be very different from others' and may be very limited in knowledge of the world. This fallacy has its basis in egocentrism, as the arguer assumes either that everyone is the exact same as they are, or that their experiences are better or more accurate than anyone else's.

Anecdotes can be very useful for illustrating an argument, but not for being the basis of an argument. This fallacy is sometimes called "misleading vividness" because a personal experience may seem so vivid that it feels reasonable to believe it without question.

"I don't trust studies and statistics, only what I see with my own eyes."

"I don't get sick even though I've never had any shots. Vaccinations are pointless and no one needs to get them."

"I was raised by strict parents and I ended up getting accepted to a prestigious college, so a strict upbringing is definitely the best way to raise kids."

"I didn't have any calculators when I was your age and had to learn how to do all math by hand, so you should too."

Anecdotal Fallacy is a sub-fallacy of...

Informal
Fallacy

Faulty
Generalization

Cherry Picking

Circular Reasoning

Trying to prove a point only by repeating or rephrasing that same point.

Circular Reasoning uses its lure to catch prey, but ends up chasing after its own lure instead. It ends up going in circles and catching nothing, but it rarely notices or cares.

Circular reasoning is also known as "*circulus in probando* (circular in proving)", "circular logic", and "begging the question".

This fallacy has a premise that is the same as its conclusion, thus the arguer tries to justify their claim by doing nothing more than restating it. Because this claim is often rephrased in different words, it can be difficult for others to notice the repetition. Circular reasoning can occasionally be seen in paradoxes, as they often play on a circular, never-ending structure.

This fallacy is sometimes used when the arguer feels that a statement is self-explanatory and does not need to be supported by evidence, or by accident because the arguer is unused to questioning the reasoning behind their own views.

"This is true because that is true, and that is true because this is true."

"You can find the new café by looking for the big oak tree. If you can't spot the big oak tree, try looking for the café, the tree is right next to it."

"Of course I'm right—I can't possibly be wrong."

"If it's against the law, then of course it's bad. That's why it's against the law in the first place!"

"This soothing tea cures anxiety thanks to its calming benefits."

Circular Reasoning is a sub-fallacy of...

Informal
Fallacy

False Dilemma

Implying there are only two possible choices in a situation when there are actually more.

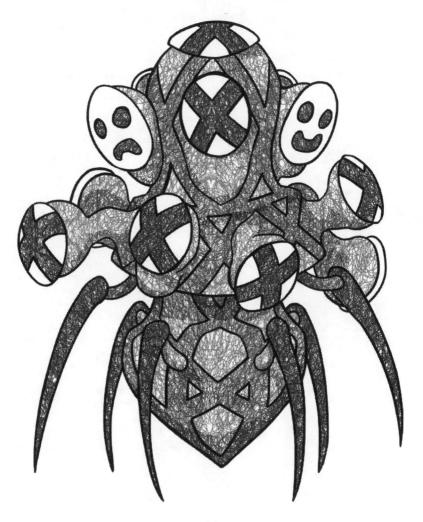

False Dilemma is a master of illusion. It narrows your view of the world until you think that everything is either black or white. Simple choices are easier for it to control.

False Dilemma is also known as "denying a conjunct", "black-or-white fallacy", "false dichotomy", and "either-or fallacy".

This fallacy occurs when the arguer assumes there are only two possible outcomes to a problem, forcing the opponent to choose one instead of considering other options. If the arguer is used to seeing things in black-or-white, they may automatically think there are limited options to choose from. However, this fallacy may also be used to intentionally manipulate the opponent.

Despite the name, an argument with three or more choices can still be considered a False Dilemma so long as at least one choice is excluded. There are mixed views over whether this fallacy is considered formal or informal.

"You can't do homework and watch TV at the same time. You're watching TV right now, which means you're not doing your homework."

"If you're not voting Republican, then clearly you must be voting Democrat."

"You're either with us or against us."

"If you don't agree to debate with me, that means you are afraid because you know you'll be proven wrong."

"If you're not fighting in the war, you're just as bad as the enemies."

False Dilemma is a sub-fallacy of...

Informal
Fallacy

Argument from Ignorance

Insisting that something is either true or false solely because it cannot be proven otherwise.

Argument from Ignorance likes to say whatever it wants, so long as you are unable to prove it wrong. It likes to pretend it is wise but would actually rather not know the truth.

Argument from Ignorance is also known as "*argumentum ad ignorantiam*" and "appeal to ignorance".

This fallacy occurs when the arguer makes a claim that lacks evidence and, if challenged, declares that the opponent is solely responsible for providing proof to the contrary. This is commonly referred to as "shifting the burden of proof", and has the result of pushing all of the work onto the opponent while at the same time making them look bad.

"Ignorance" can refer to anything ranging from humankind's limited knowledge in general, to just the arguer's individual knowledge that is lacking due to a refusal to believe, learn more, or investigate further.

"There's no evidence that ghosts don't exist, so they must be real."

"If a tree fell in the forest and no one was around to hear it, then obviously it wouldn't have made any sound."

"It's fine if I drive over the speed limit. Sure, there are people who crash because of speeding, but there are also people who speed all the time and are fine. Who's to say that I'm not one of them?"

"If you can't prove your beliefs, then they aren't true. It's impossible for something to be true without evidence."

Argument from Ignorance is a sub-fallacy of...

Informal
Fallacy

False Dilemma

Argument from Incredulity

Denying the possibility of something because it is hard to imagine it as being true.

Argument from Incredulity does not have much of an imagination. It would rather just stay where it is and let its head melt away, believing whatever it wants to.

Argument from Incredulity is also known as "argument by lack of imagination" and "argument from personal incredulity".

This fallacy occurs when the arguer makes a claim assuming that something is or is not the case based on how well the arguer personally is able to imagine it as being such. If the arguer cannot understand why something might exist or be the case, they may therefore insist that it must be impossible. This may be due to personal disbelief in a subject, or it may simply be that the arguer does not want to think past their initial impressions.

Since Argument from Incredulity rejects an argument based on a lack of evidence, the fallacy is considered a specific type of Argument from Ignorance.

"It's not possible for humans to have built the pyramids, given the lack of technology at the time. It must have been aliens or something."

"They said they're going to put people on Mars, but that's just ridiculous, it can't be done."

"I heard that a bee has wings that are too small to get its body off the ground. It shouldn't be possible for bees to be able to fly."

"I can't imagine people possibly being happy without a significant other, so it must be that they're lying when they say they aren't interested in dating."

Argument from Incredulity is a sub-fallacy of...

Informal
Fallacy

False Dilemma

Argument from
Ignorance

Nirvana Fallacy

Rejecting a claim in favor of an idealized
alternative that is too unrealistic to exist

Nirvana Fallacy holds all things up to high standards. It
sees ideals and potential. It is positive to the point of
irrationality, and rejects anything that is less than perfect.

Nirvana Fallacy is also known as "perfectionist's fallacy" and "perfect solution fallacy".

This fallacy occurs when the arguer rejects a claim that has any faults or disadvantages to it, insisting that it needs to be perfect and solve every possible problem presented. The arguer's view is idealized to the extent that it is unfeasible and could not happen in reality. However, to others, this idealized solution may appear to be overwhelmingly better than the more realistic claim presented by the opponent, and thus may give the illusion that the arguer has a more successful claim.

Since Nirvana Fallacy rejects a claim in favor of only one other potential option, it is a type of False Dilemma.

"People will still kill each other even without guns. There's no point in stricter gun control if people continue to get murdered."

"Even with restrictions, criminals will find a way to buy guns. Guns should be banned worldwide."

"There's no point in treating people nicely in life. We're all going to die eventually anyway, so it doesn't matter in the end."

"Vaccines don't work 100% of the time, so why even bother at all?"

"This medicine has side effects, so I refuse to take it."

Nirvana Fallacy is a sub-fallacy of...

Informal
Fallacy

False Dilemma

Fallacy Fallacy

Dismissing an argument's worth solely
because it is a logical fallacy.

Fallacy Fallacy tricks those who think they are smart and
know better than others. They make for excellent prey.
Sometimes it's best not to be too self-assured.

Fallacy Fallacy is also known as "*argumentum ad logicam*" and "fallacist's fallacy".

This fallacy occurs when the arguer claims their opponent is using a fallacy, and uses this as grounds to declare the entire argument to be wrong. Just because an argument is flawed does not necessarily mean that everything about it is incorrect. It is possible that a claim or view is right even if it was communicated poorly. Fallacy Fallacy is common among students who are new to the world of fallacies and have not yet mastered its intricacies.

Many fallacies vary depending on the situation and individual technicalities, so it is important to examine arguments thoroughly before deciding if they are fallacious.

"This politician just called his opponent 'stupid'. How can you support someone who uses character assassination as a tactic?"

"You're making a 'slippery slope' argument, so there's no way it can be right."

"I'm pretty sure what you just said is a fallacy. Why don't we end this conversation here before you embarass yourself even further?"

"I'm making a 'two wrongs make a right' fallacy? Yeah, well, you're making a 'fallacy fallacy', so I don't see why you think you're somehow better than me."

Fallacy Fallacy is a sub-fallacy of...

Formal Fallacy

Non Sequitur

Logical Fallacy
Taxonomy

Formal

Non Sequitur

Gambler's
Fallacy

Hot Hand
Fallacy

Masked Man
Fallacy

Denying the
Antecedent

Affirming the
Consequent

Fallacy Fallacy

Informal

Red Herring

Special
Pleading

Two Wrongs
Make a Right

Genetic
Fallacy

Moving the
Goalposts

Appeal to
Emotion

Etymological
Fallacy

Appeal to
Novelty

Appeal to
Authority

Bandwagon
Fallacy

Appeal to
Tradition

Straw Man

Ad Hominem

Ad Iram

Informal

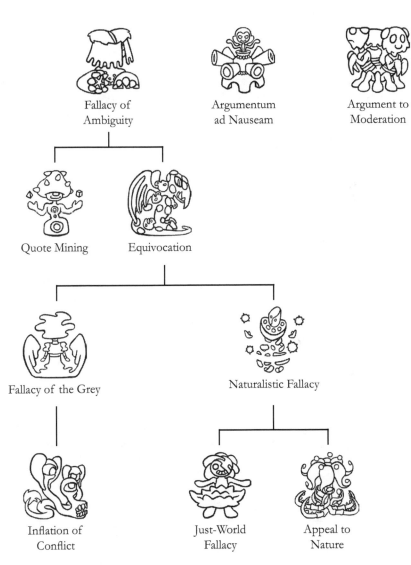

Fallacy of
Ambiguity

Argumentum
ad Nauseam

Argument to
Moderation

Quote Mining

Equivocation

Fallacy of the Grey

Naturalistic Fallacy

Inflation of
Conflict

Just-World
Fallacy

Appeal to
Nature

Informal

Sunk-Cost
Fallacy

Faulty
Generalization

Circular
Reasoning

Toupée Fallacy

Slippery Slope

Questionable
Cause

Tokenism

Fallacy of
Composition

Fallacy of
Division

Faulty Analogy

Over-
simplification

Association
Fallacy

Fallacy of
Equity

Informal

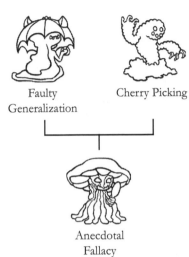

Faulty
Generalization

Cherry Picking

False Dilemma

Anecdotal
Fallacy

Argument
from Ignorance

Nirvana
Fallacy

Argument from
Incredulity

Fallacy Index

Made in the USA
Las Vegas, NV
15 August 2023

76127197R00074